PIRATES

Rupert Matthews

p

CONTENTS

This is a Parragon Book
First published in 2006

Parragon
Queen Street House
4 Queen Street
Bath BA1 1HE, UK

Copyright © Parragon Books Ltd 2006

Produced by

Calcium
New Brook House
385 Alfreton Road
Nottingham
NG7 5LR

British Library Cataloguing-in-Publication Data

A catalogue record for this book is available from
the British Library.

ISBN 1-40545-102-5

Printed in China

Designer
Paul Myerscough

Illustrator
Terry Riley (SGA)

Cartoonist
Peter Wilks (SGA)

Editor
Sarah Eason

Consultant
Bob Rees

PIRATES!

PIRATES ARE PEOPLE who sail the seas searching for ships to capture and rob. The most famous pirates in history were the pirates of the Caribbean. These were English and French sailors who robbed Spanish ships carrying gold from mines in South America. These pirates sailed the seas off the coasts of North and South America from 1620 to 1740.

YOU MUST BE JOKING!
In 1689 a group of French pirates stole everything they could carry from the Spanish city of Cartagena – including the city's pets!

CAN YOU BELIEVE IT?
Pirate captains kept all the loot.

NO. The captain and crew agreed how they would divide up stolen treasure before they went to sea.

Under attack
Pirates attacked merchant ships whenever they could. These were unarmed ships that carried goods. Pirates only fought other warships if they had to.

NO PEACE BEYOND THE LINE
In 1494 the Catholic Pope declared that all land and sea beyond a line in the Atlantic Ocean belonged to Spain. This was called the Treaty of Tordisillas. The Spanish began to attack foreign ships that sailed beyond the line. The crews of these ships fought back, and began to steal gold from Spanish ships.

Tordisillas Line

South America

Atlantic Ocean

BUCCANEERS!

YES. Before they began to rob Spanish ships, English and French sailors in the Caribbean sold smoked meat called 'boucan' to passing ships. This was how they got the name 'boucanier'.

DURING THE 1620s, many English and French sailors settled on the island of Haiti. They were known as 'boucaniers'. But the Spanish claimed Haiti for themselves and didn't want anyone else to live there. In the 1630s the Spanish attacked Haiti. The boucaniers escaped to the island of Tortuga. From then on they became pirates (buccaneers) and attacked Spanish ships carrying gold.

THE PIRATE AUTHOR
In 1683 the pirate Alexander Esquemeling wrote a book about his adventures. 'Buccaneers of America' was an instant best-seller. Esquemeling made more money from the book than he had done as a pirate! The book is still in print even today and many of our pirate legends are based on it.

Armed and ready
Even if a ship surrendered, pirates would always board it fully armed.

YOU MUST BE JOKING!
The pirate Bartolomeo el Portuguese captured a Spanish ship in 1655. He thought it was full of gold, but found it was carrying lots of chocolate instead!

PIRATES USED FAST, heavily armed ships. They needed to be able to catch up with merchant ships, then defeat them if they fought back. Some pirates preferred to have small ships so that they could hide in narrow inlets and creeks. Others chose larger ships with more guns. The ship needed enough space to carry food for the crew, ammunition for the guns and to store all the loot the pirates stole.

CAN YOU BELIEVE IT?
Pirates built their own ships.

NO. Most pirates stole ships. If a pirate captured a ship better than his own, he would sell his ship and keep the new one.

CAMOUFLAGE
The hulls of a pirate ship were often painted green so that they would blend in with the green land of the creeks and inlets where the ship hid.

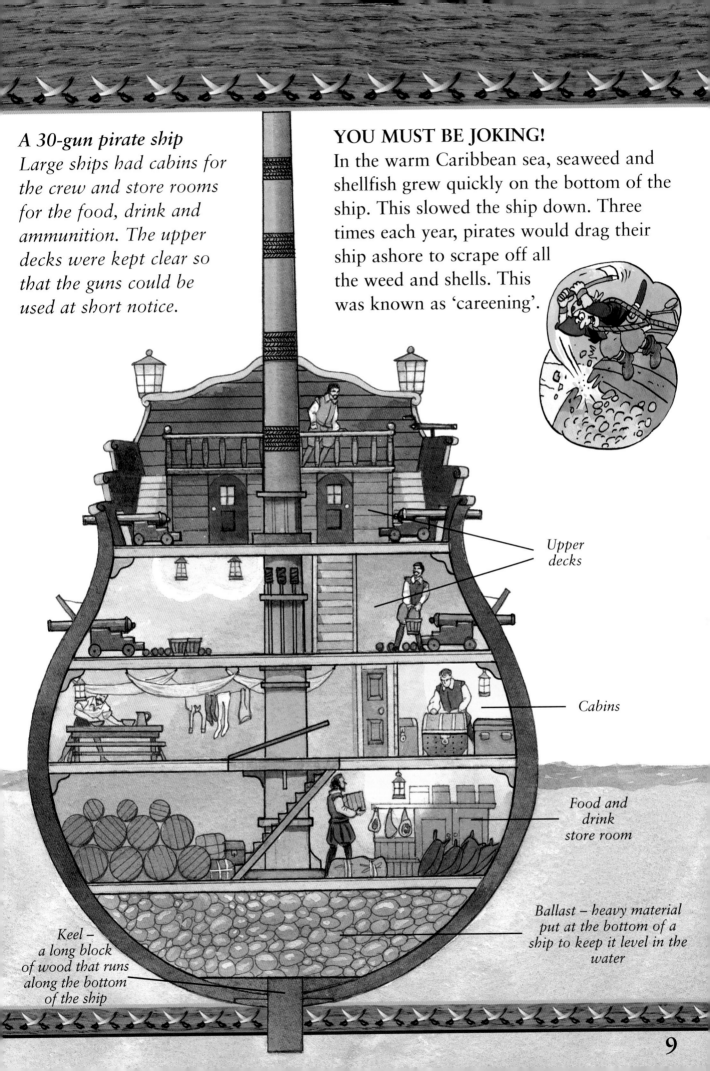

A 30-gun pirate ship
Large ships had cabins for the crew and store rooms for the food, drink and ammunition. The upper decks were kept clear so that the guns could be used at short notice.

YOU MUST BE JOKING!
In the warm Caribbean sea, seaweed and shellfish grew quickly on the bottom of the ship. This slowed the ship down. Three times each year, pirates would drag their ship ashore to scrape off all the weed and shells. This was known as 'careening'.

Upper decks

Cabins

Food and drink store room

Ballast – heavy material put at the bottom of a ship to keep it level in the water

Keel – a long block of wood that runs along the bottom of the ship

THE ARTICLES

BEFORE SETTING OUT on a voyage, a pirate crew would sign 'Articles'. These were rules drawn up by the captain and crew. They described how the ship would be run, how treasure would be divided up and what punishments would be given to pirates who broke the rules. Some Articles were long lists of rules, others were just a few points.

CAN YOU BELIEVE IT?
Pirates made prisoners walk the plank.

NO. Very few pirates killed their prisoners because they were worth more if they held them hostage for a ransom.

Signing Articles
Most pirates were able to read and sign their name, but those who couldn't just made a mark instead.

MAROONING

Apart from death, the worst punishment pirates gave each other was 'marooning'. This meant leaving a pirate on his own on a far-away island. Alexander Selkirk (better known as Robinson Crusoe) was marooned on Juan Fernandez in 1705. He was rescued in 1709. The famous book 'Robinson Crusoe' is based on his story.

YOU MUST BE JOKING!

If the crew felt a captain was making bad decisions, they could hold a vote to choose a new one.

THE PIRATE KNIGHT

HENRY MORGAN was the richest and most powerful pirate of all. He was born in South Wales in 1635. By 1662 he was the captain of a pirate ship which sailed from Port Royal, Jamaica. His greatest adventure was to gather an army of 2,000 pirates and 33 ships to capture the city of Panama in 1671. Panama was then the richest Spanish city in South America. In 1675 Morgan retired. He invested his loot wisely so that he had plenty of money to live on.

City treasures
Morgan captured several cities and lots of ships. He threatened to burn down the cities, unless the Spanish gave him lots of money.

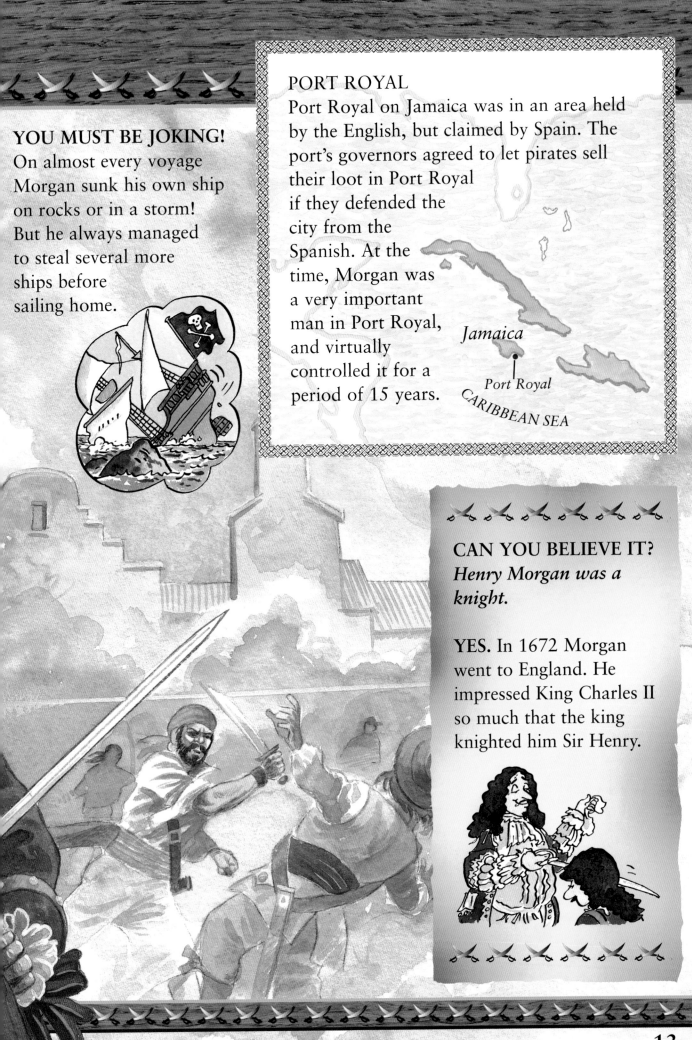

YOU MUST BE JOKING!

On almost every voyage Morgan sunk his own ship on rocks or in a storm! But he always managed to steal several more ships before sailing home.

PORT ROYAL

Port Royal on Jamaica was in an area held by the English, but claimed by Spain. The port's governors agreed to let pirates sell their loot in Port Royal if they defended the city from the Spanish. At the time, Morgan was a very important man in Port Royal, and virtually controlled it for a period of 15 years.

Jamaica

Port Royal

CARIBBEAN SEA

CAN YOU BELIEVE IT?

Henry Morgan was a knight.

YES. In 1672 Morgan went to England. He impressed King Charles II so much that the king knighted him Sir Henry.

PIRATE WEAPONS

THE MOST IMPORTANT weapons on a pirate ship were the guns. These weapons fired a solid ball of iron weighing 15kg over distances of 4km. A single shot could stop a small ship in its tracks. Pirates also used the guns to fire two cannon balls linked together by an iron chain. These tore apart sails and rigging, bringing even big ships to a halt.

Cannon fire
Pirates would hope to damage a ship and make it helpless, ready for them to board.

PIRATE FIREARMS
If a ship did not surrender at once, pirates would get close enough to jump onboard and fight the crew with swords and guns. Pistols and muskets took a long time to reload and did not work at all if they got wet. Most pirates would carry two pistols *and* a sharp, curved sword called a 'cutlass'.

A musket, gunpowder and shot

YOU MUST BE JOKING!

Pirate captains often designed their own pirate flag, called a 'Jolly Roger'. Each tried to make his the most terrifying of all.

CAN YOU BELIEVE IT?

Pirates carried a cutlass at all times.

NO. They were given out only when a fight was about to start. Weapons onboard pirate ships were usually kept locked away so that the pirates did not use them in fights among themselves.

THE PIRATE EXPLORER

YOU MUST BE JOKING!
Dampier was so skilled at map-making and navigation that the British Royal Navy made him a captain in 1699 – even though he had once been a pirate.

WILLIAM DAMPIER first went to sea when he was still a boy. He spent many years learning to read charts and maps, and became one of the world's most skilled navigators.

CAN YOU BELIEVE IT?
Dampier was the first man to sail around the world three times.

YES. Between 1683 and 1711 he made three complete journeys around the world.

Dampier discovered many new lands, including much of western Australia. He became a pirate in 1676 and took part in a number of raids on Spanish ships. On his last journey, he rescued Alexander Selkirk (Robinson Crusoe) from Juan Fernandez Island. Dampier later wrote a book about his adventures.

Map-making
Dampier took careful measurements to find out his ship's position. Then he added the information to his charts.

THE ART OF NAVIGATION

In the 1700s, a navigator used a quadrant, compass and hour glass to find his way across the oceans. At the time, these were important navigation tools. Good navigators also used a ship's speed and the amount of time it had been sailing to work out their position, but even skilled men such as Dampier were often wrong.

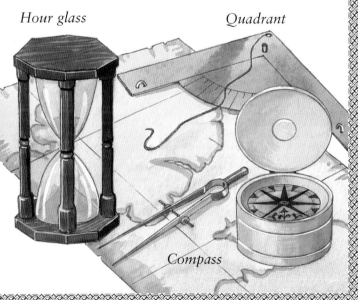

Hour glass

Quadrant

Compass

LIFE ON BOARD

PIRATES SPENT most of their time at sea doing very little! Only a few men were needed to work the ship in good weather, and none were needed to fire the guns, except in action. Pirates would often play games with cards or with dice. Some would play music and dance. Others spent time carving model ships, or telling each other stories about their adventures.

CAN YOU BELIEVE IT?
Pirates knew how to sew.

YES. All pirates needed to mend their clothes and the ship's sails. Pirates loved showy clothes and often stitched gold or silver thread on to their coats and jackets.

Below deck
The space inside a ship was small and crowded. Pirates had to share cabins, in which they also cooked, ate and slept.

PIRATE CLOTHES
Pirates lived in hot, rainy areas. During good weather, they wore cotton shirts over loose trousers. In wet weather, they wore a cloak smeared with tar to keep the water out. Many tied a cloth around their head to soak up sweat, and wore a hat with a wide brim to keep the sun out of their eyes. Most pirates kept a wool coat or suit to look smart when they went ashore.

YOU MUST BE JOKING!
Keeping food fresh on a long voyage was difficult. Most ships carried biscuits, which didn't rot, but were often full of small beetles called 'weevils'!

CAN YOU BELIEVE IT?
*Before becoming a pirate
Mary Read was a soldier.*

YES. As a young woman Mary Read married a soldier. She joined the army, disguised as a man, to be with him. She served for ten years. When her husband died she became a sailor, and later joined a crew of pirates.

A FEW WOMEN became pirates. The most famous were Anne Bonny and Mary Read. These women sailed with the pirate captain Calico Jack Rackham for over two years. They dressed as women most of the time, but wore men's clothing for fighting. Anne and Mary were caught and put on trial in Jamaica in 1720. They escaped hanging, but were still sent to prison.

HOW WOMEN BECAME PIRATES

The women who became pirates probably did so for the same reasons as men – they wanted money. Anne Bonny became a pirate to be with Calico Jack Rackham, who was her boyfriend. Mary Read became a pirate after the ship in which she was a passenger was captured by Calico Jack Rackham. She so impressed him with her sword skills that he asked her to join his crew!

YOU MUST BE JOKING! When they were finally captured, Mary and Anne fought much harder than any of the men in their crew.

Famous fighters
Anne and Mary were both great swordswomen. Mary, in particular, was well known as a fearsome and skilled fighter.

YOU MUST BE JOKING!
Frenchman Jean le Vasseur
was sent to Tortuga to get
rid of the pirates. Instead,
he let them stay – as long as
they gave him 10 percent of
their loot.

AT THE END of a voyage pirates would swarm ashore with their loot. Harbours such as Port Royal or Tortuga had plenty of places for pirates to spend money. They bought fancy clothes from tailors, and lots of jewellery.

Pirates especially liked to buy richly decorated weapons. Some pirates ran out of money in a few days, others after weeks. Very few pirates saved any of the money they made.

Taverns and farms
Pirates spent lots of time ashore drinking in taverns. Some were farmers who went back to their farms when they weren't at sea.

PIRATE HAVENS
All pirates needed a port where they could sell their loot and buy supplies. The island of Haiti and Campeche Bay on the Mexican coast both had ports that were popular pirate havens. Campeche Bay also had many small bays in which pirates could hide their ships.

Campeche Bay

Haiti

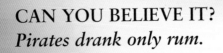

CAN YOU BELIEVE IT?
Pirates drank only rum.

NO. Many pirates preferred to drink wine. After each voyage, Henry Morgan bought a large barrel of red wine. Then he sat on the dockside drinking with his friends until the wine was gone.

23

THE MOST FAMOUS PIRATE

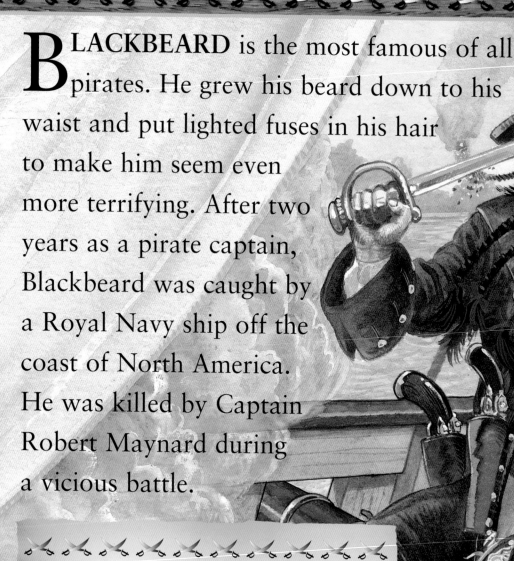

BLACKBEARD is the most famous of all pirates. He grew his beard down to his waist and put lighted fuses in his hair to make him seem even more terrifying. After two years as a pirate captain, Blackbeard was caught by a Royal Navy ship off the coast of North America. He was killed by Captain Robert Maynard during a vicious battle.

CAN YOU BELIEVE IT?
Blackbeard even robbed his own crew.

YES. In July 1718, Blackbeard was returning from a successful voyage with a lot of loot. The ship ran aground, so Blackbeard loaded the treasure into a boat and rowed off, promising to return for his crew. He never came back!

The last fight
Armed with seven pistols and a cutlass, Blackbeard fought until he was shot dead.

YOU MUST BE JOKING!
Blackbeard's favourite drink was rum mixed with gunpowder!

A PRICE ON HIS HEAD
Pirates became so troublesome in the 1700s that a reward was offered to anyone who could capture them. In 1718 a price of £15 was offered for any pirate caught alive, and £40 for a pirate captain. Some pirates were allowed to go free if they handed over their ship and weapons.

PIRATE TREASURE

CAN YOU BELIEVE IT?
Pirates shared out the loot equally.

NO. It was divided into shares. Ordinary
pirates got one share of all the loot. Skilled
men, such as carpenters, got one and a half
shares. The captain might get as
much as four shares.

Burying treasure
*Some pirates may have buried treasure,
but most spent the money as soon as they got it.*

OVER THE YEARS pirates stole huge amounts of money and treasure. In 1720 a pirate called Captain Edward England captured a ship carrying gold worth around £7 million in today's money. Most pirates spent their money very quickly, although some saved it to buy farms or taverns. Some pirate treasure was buried. It is said that Blackbeard buried his loot the day before he was killed, and Captain Kidd buried 100,000 gold coins somewhere. Neither treasure has ever been found.

PIRATE LOOT
Pirates stole almost anything. They preferred things that could be sold quickly and easily for cash, such as gold and jewels. If there was nothing valuable onboard a ship to steal, the pirates would take rice, flour or even coal. Sometimes they stole the ship itself.

YOU MUST BE JOKING!
The first US dollar was based on the pirate coin, called a 'Piece of Eight'.

THE WARTIME PIRATE

WHEN BRITAIN went to war with France in 1688, the king told British captains to attack French ships. In return, they were allowed to keep some of the treasure the French ships carried. Captain Kidd went too far and attacked the *Quetta Merchant*, a ship owned by the Emperor of India. Kidd said he attacked the ship because it held French goods. He stole everything onboard.

Stealing treasure
Kidd was later put on trial for attacking the Quetta Merchant *and stealing all its treasure.*

FINANCING A VOYAGE
Pirates often borrowed money to buy their ships and weapons. Kidd borrowed £6,000 from men such as the Duke of Shrewsbury and different London businessmen. He also paid £1,200 himself.

YOU MUST BE JOKING!

Captain Kidd was eventually hanged for the murder of a crewman. Kidd hit him on the head with a bucket during an argument.

CAN YOU BELIEVE IT?

Kidd only made one voyage as a pirate.

YES. Before he became a pirate, Kidd had been the captain of a merchant ship for many years. He was 50 years old when he captured the *Quetta Merchant*, on his first and only pirate voyage.

THE LAST PIRATES

THE EARLY PIRATES had helped to protect English and French areas from attack by the Spanish, but in 1715 general peace was agreed between all countries. Merchants now wanted their ships protected from pirates. In 1717 King George I of England gave all pirates a year to surrender, after which the Royal Navy was sent to hunt them down. Any pirate then found guilty was to be hanged.

CAN YOU BELIEVE IT?
The bodies of pirates were left hanging in harbours.

YES. After 1700 the bodies of hanged pirates were placed in iron cages and hung beside harbours as a warning to stop people becoming pirates.

Pirates under attack
After 1718 British warships were ordered to attack and sink any pirate ships they found.

YOU MUST BE JOKING!

The pirate captain Edward Low was sacked by his own pirate crew – he was too cruel even for them!

PIRATES TODAY

Pirates didn't just vanish after the 1700s. There were Algerian pirates in the Mediterranean until the 1830s, and pirates sailed the coast of China until 1860. In the 1980s there were new pirate attacks in the Caribbean, which were linked to the drugs trade. In the 1990s there were many attacks by armed men in fast motorboats in Indonesia and the Philippines. Pirates are still a problem in this area even today.

INDEX